2695 2/04

What Are
Wedges?

by Helen Frost

Consulting Editor: Gail Saunders-Smith, Ph.D.

Consultant: Philip W. Hammer, Ph.D.
Assistant Director of Education
American Institute of Physics

Pebble Books

an imprint of Capstone Press
Mankato, Minnesota

Pebble Books are published by Capstone Press
151 Good Counsel Drive, P.O. Box 669, Mankato, Minnesota 56002
http://www.capstone-press.com

Library of Congress Cataloging-in-Publication Data
Frost, Helen, 1949–
    What are wedges? / by Helen Frost.
    p. cm.—(Looking at simple machines)
    Includes bibliographical references (p. 23) and index.
    ISBN 0-7368-0849-3
    1. Wedges—Juvenile literature. [1. Wedges.] I.Title. II. Series.
TJ1201.W44 F76 2001
621.9'9—dc21

                                00-009871

Summary: Simple text and photographs present wedges and their function as a simple machine.

Note to Parents and Teachers

The Looking at Simple Machines series supports national science standards for units on understanding work, force, and tools. This book describes wedges and illustrates how they make work easier. The photographs support early readers in understanding the text. This book also introduces early readers to subject-specific vocabulary words, which are defined in the Words to Know section. Early readers may need assistance to read some words and to use the Table of Contents, Words to Know, Read More, Internet Sites, and Index/Word List sections of the book.

Table of Contents

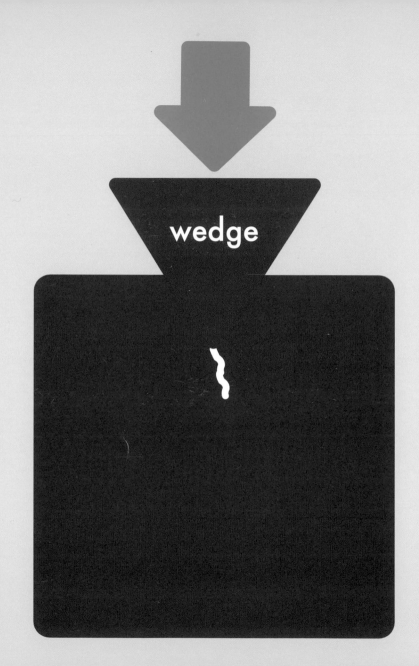

wedge

4

A wedge is
a simple machine.

A wedge has a narrow edge and a wide edge.

The narrow edge of a wedge cuts a small gap.

force

Force is put on the wide edge of a wedge.

The wedge makes
the gap bigger.

14

Wedges cut or
separate objects.

Teeth are wedges.

A zipper is a wedge.

A knife is a wedge.

Words to Know

force—a push or a pull on an object; force makes objects start moving, speed up, change direction, or stop moving.

knife—a tool with a sharp blade; people use knives to cut objects such as food.

separate—to part or divide something

simple machine—a tool that makes work easier; work is using a force to move an object across a distance; inclined planes, levers, and pulleys are examples of simple machines; a wedge is a type of inclined plane.

teeth—the hard, white parts of the mouth; teeth are used for biting and chewing food.

wedge—an object with a narrow edge and a wide edge that is a simple machine

Read More

Armentrout, Patricia. *The Wedge.* Simple Devices. Vero Beach, Fla.: Rourke, 1997.

Oxlade, Chris. *Machines.* Young Scientist Concepts and Projects. Milwaukee: Gareth Stevens, 1998.

Rush, Caroline. *Slopes.* Simple Science. Austin, Texas: Raintree Steck-Vaughn, 1997.

Welsbacher, Anne. *Wedges.* Understanding Simple Machines. Mankato, Minn.: Bridgestone Books, 2001.

Internet Sites

Simple Machines
http://sln.fi.edu/qa97/spotlight3/spotlight3.html

The Wedge
http://www.robinsonresearch.com/TECHNOL/
the_wedge.htm

Wedge
http://library.thinkquest.org/J002079F/wedge.htm

Index/Word List

Word Count: 60
Early-Intervention Level: 9

Editorial Credits
Martha E. H. Rustad, editor; Kia Bielke, cover designer and illustrator; Kimberly
  Danger, photo researcher

Photo Credits
Capstone Press/CG Book Printers, 20
Jack Glisson, 1, 16
Kimberly Danger, cover, 6, 8, 10, 12, 14
Visuals Unlimited/Jeff J. Daly, 18

The author thanks the children's section staff at the Allen County Public Library
in Fort Wayne, Indiana, for research assistance. The author also thanks Josué
Njock Libii, Ph.D, Associate Professor of Mechanical Engineering at Indiana
University–Purdue University.